FARMERS, TEMPLES
AND TOMBS

Farmers, Temples and Tombs

Scotland in the Neolithic and Early Bronze Age

Gordon Barclay

Series editor: Gordon Barclay

CANONGATE BOOKS

with

HISTORIC SCOTLAND

THE MAKING
OF SCOTLAND

Series editor:
Gordon Barclay

Other titles available:

WILD HARVESTERS:
The First People in Scotland

SETTLEMENT AND SACRIFICE:
The Later Prehistoric People
of Scotland

A GATHERING OF EAGLES:
Scenes from Roman Scotland

First published in Great Britain in 1998
by Canongate Books Ltd, 14 High
Street, Edinburgh EH1 1TE

British Library Cataloguing-in-Publication Data
A catalogue record for this book is available on request
from the British Library

ISBN 0 86241 780 5

Series Design:
James Hutcheson, Canongate Books

Printed and bound by
GraphyCems

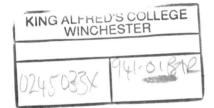

Previous page
Excavation at Clava, near Inverness
HISTORIC SCOTLAND

Contents

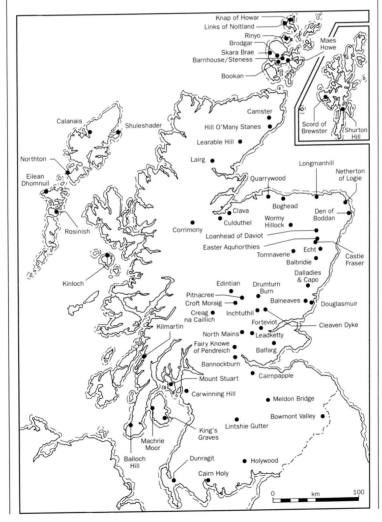

Location map
Sites mentioned
within text

Misconceptions of the Neolithic

Many people have the strangest ideas about what happened in this period of history, assuming that the ceremonial sites of the period were built by the druids, who turn up in history over 2000 years later.

Out of the Wildwood

This book describes the beginnings and development of the farming communities of Scotland until about 1500 BC, how they worked the land, how they lived, how they buried their dead and how they worshipped; the things they made and exchanged; and how they transformed the landscape.

There are many misconceptions about the period, and about the monuments that were built then. Modern 'pagans' claim some of the sites discussed here - but they mistakenly impose their search for alternative beliefs on the artefacts and the people of the past.

In the pages that follow I will be describing great monuments and simple settlements – farms, pots, metalwork. In books about the past we can sometimes lose touch with the fact that sites were built and used, farms run, and metalwork and pots made, by people; people with children and other responsibilities; people sometimes far-sighted and sensible, sometimes caring only for the short term and just as capable of making mistakes as any of us. They were indeed like us in many ways - certainly physically, although they will have had ideas about the world and the way it worked that might seem very alien to us. They cared for their ill and old, and buried the dead with great care; they designed and built great structures. Archaeology can only show us fleeting glimpses of the day-to-day lives of people, and we see them through the eyes of our modern culture. In the pages that follow think of real people. They were a little shorter than us on average. They suffered like us from the pain of injury and illness, without the resources of modern medicine, but with folk-medicine, perhaps of great sophistication. They were certainly at greater risk from death by accident and illness, had a life expectancy of 20 to 30 years less than ours, and would have had a far higher rate of child mortality. But forget any idea that they lived in a 'golden age' in harmony with their environment. They, like us, were capable of damaging their environment, and we have evidence of the disastrous consequences of their actions, for example soil erosion caused by deforestation, in prehistory.

It was in the Neolithic period that the process of creating the modern 'cultural' landscape really began. Before the first farmers began cutting the wood for agriculture, woodland covered most of the country below the tree-line (the height above which trees will not grow); Britain now has relatively little woodland compared to other European countries. The change from one state to the other has been the subject of what the ecologist Oliver Rackham has described as 'countryside myths' - the loss of woodland has been blamed on the Romans, the warfare of the Vikings (who certainly had little impact), the iron masters of the eighteenth century (who actually had more to gain from managing the woods, as they did in reality), and ship-building for the Napoleonic Wars. While all no doubt played a greater or lesser part in the history of Scottish woodlands, the loss of woodland has been caused almost entirely by one activity - the clearing of trees to provide farmland, both for growing crops and for pasture.

There is evidence of human management of the woodlands that existed before the beginning of farming - areas may have been burned or cleared to aid hunting. What is valued is protected and much woodland was preserved and managed throughout history to provide timber and other woodland products. But the clearance of the wildwood was more than half completed long before the Romans set foot upon this island - the first farmers described in this book began the process of turning a wild landscape into a domesticated one by ordering the land and cutting down the trees. This process of change has resulted in the landscape we see about us, from the sea shore to the high hills, which is far from 'natural'.

Many books on the prehistory of Scotland have perhaps over-emphasised areas where stone structures of the period survive – mainly in the uplands and the Northern Isles – and neglected areas that were of just as much importance in the past, and possibly more densely settled, in the lowlands of mainland Scotland. This book is about *all* of Scotland. I also refer to what was happening in the rest of Britain and in Ireland at this time. Even though prehistoric remains in the lowlands may not be as obvious at first sight as in the areas of stone building, they *are* there, in great profusion.

DATES

For over 40 years archaeologists have been able to use a scientific process called radiocarbon dating to tell the age of organic material (such as wood, charcoal, textiles). Radiocarbon dating does not provide real calendar dates; to provide these the raw determinations have to be calibrated using radiocarbon dates taken from materials of known age (for example wood from long-lived trees where counting tree-rings can give us an exact age). Throughout this book I have used dates based upon calibrated radiocarbon determinations – for example 'around 4000 BC'. For more information on radiocarbon dating see the 'Further Reading' list at the end of the book.

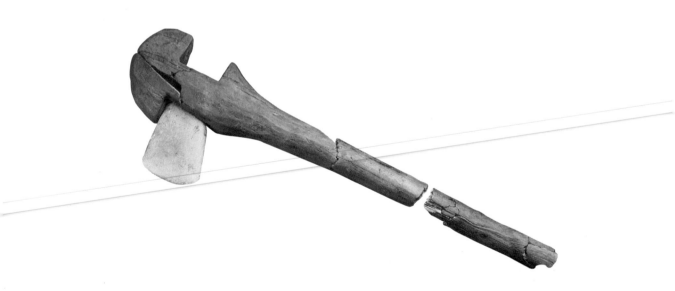

Shuleshader Axe

This Neolithic axe was found, complete with its handle – a unique discovery – in a bog on Lewis. This find shows the importance of wooden artefacts, which are rarely preserved.

NATIONAL MUSEUMS OF SCOTLAND

What is the Neolithic?

The Neolithic (the word means 'new stone age') is the period of the first farmers in Britain. Around 4000 BC, for the first time, people began to use domesticated animals and plants (both introduced from continental Europe) as food sources. New technology was also introduced – pottery and polished stone axes (although some of these were found earlier in Wales). Around the same time people began to build large tombs for burial.

What came before?

By around 8000 BC the last ice sheets of the most recent Ice Age had melted and the climate was warming rapidly. The ice in large glaciers can be more than 2km (over 1 mile) deep, accumulating on high, cooler ground and moving downwards and outwards to lower, warmer levels; in doing this they exert colossal stresses on the underlying land, grinding out deep valleys and wearing down hills. The ice sheets over Scotland comprised billions of tonnes of frozen water. As they melted, vast quantities of silts, sands and gravels created by the grinding effect of the glaciers on the underlying rock, were washed over the lower land, transforming the landscape into a general shape we would recognise today. However, it was a devastated landscape of gravel, sand, and lochs. There was no soil and at first nothing lived there; in some areas boulders would have been thickly strewn across the land.

A Glaciated Landscape

This scene is in Iceland. Scotland looked like this 10,000 years ago, and only hundreds of generations of natural processes and hard work can turn this into the landscape we know today.
NOEL FOJUT

Over the following hundreds and thousands of years the soils developed by natural processes (such as water action, frost, chemical reaction), reflecting the type of rock or glacial outwash on which they formed. Plants colonised the land - first herbs and shrubs, such as sedges, birch, dwarf willow, juniper and the like, then denser woodland, such as oak, hazel and elm over most of the lowlands, birch, hazel and oak in the north-east, and pine and birch in the Highlands. With the trees came animals - bears, wolves, wild cattle, wild pig, squirrels, otters, hedgehogs, voles and shrews. To the coasts, rivers and lochs came fish and to the skies, birds. And finally, with the animals and the fish, came the people who hunted and fished, and gathered the products of the forest - such as nuts and fungi: the 'hunter-gatherer-fishers'. The story of these people is told in detail in Bill Finlayson's companion book in this series *Wild Harvesters*, but we must describe them briefly here, because to understand the first farmers, we must try to understand their predecessors.

These 'hunter-gatherer-fishers' exploited the natural resources of the land - they hunted large and small animals, birds, freshwater and coastal fish, and gathered shellfish in great quantities. They built complex traps for

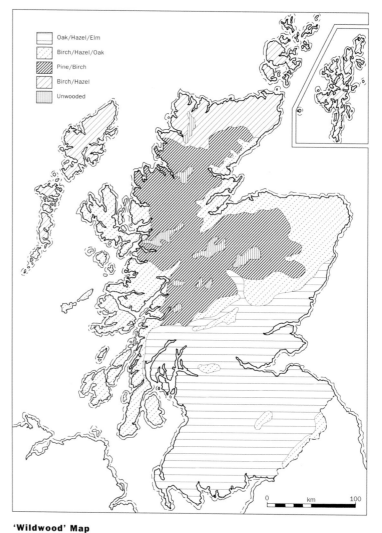

'Wildwood' Map
The makeup of the 'wildwood' after the last glaciation. *After Edwards and Whittington*

Legend:
- Oak/Hazel/Elm
- Birch/Hazel/Oak
- Pine/Birch
- Birch/Hazel
- Unwooded

fish, and skilfully fashioned tools of flint and other stones. Too often these people are still thought of as 'squat grunting savages', a misconception from the days when our ancestors preferred to believe that modern equivalents of such people, for example the native Australians, were 'lesser beings' in order to ease the theft of the natives' land by European colonists. These native peoples were not 'primitive', in the sense of stupid or simple: peoples who pursue a hunting and gathering way of life have complex social structures, ancient and sophisticated religious beliefs, traditions of occupation and use of landscapes, all preserved in oral history and traditions of story-telling. They make tools and art of great complexity. The limited evidence we have from archaeology suggests that our hunter-gatherer-fisher ancestors were just as sophisticated.

Clearing the Land

Before the first farmers, much of Scotland was covered by woodland. Around 3800 BC, however, there occurred the most widely recognised environmental event in this period - the sudden and substantial decline in the elm population of Britain and Ireland; the amount of elm pollen falling into bogs dropped by some 50 per cent. At one time this was thought to be a direct consequence of human intervention - such as the feeding of elm to animals or the felling or pollarding of trees. However, human activity alone cannot account for the vast scale of the decline and it is more likely that the reduction was caused by elm disease of the kind that has affected Britain in recent years. Pollen analysis of bogs has also recovered traces of cereal pollen some time before the elm decline, around 5000 to 4500 BC, probably indicating that farming of some kind was already going on.

What is farming?

Farming is both a system of food production, and a series of beliefs and attitudes. Reliable food production involves skilful management of animals and plants in varying conditions; the beliefs and attitudes include how people think about land and its ownership, perhaps in different ways from hunter-gatherer-fishers. Farming also necessitates different social and economic systems for the exchange of goods, customs and religious beliefs related to the cycle of the seasons. Archaeology can answer some of the questions about how farmers first tilled the fields of Britain, how they lived, something of what they believed, and how they organised their society.

There are some basic building blocks of a farming way of life and most of these were introduced into Scotland: they are *domesticated animals* - cattle (the local wild cattle were larger), sheep, goats and pigs; *domesticated plants for eating* – cereals like wheat and barley, and beans; and *domesticated plants for other uses* – for example, flax for making cloth. Not all of these are needed, as some farming societies, for example, may be based solely on the herding of cattle, with little or no planting and harvesting of crops.

The use of local, naturally occurring foods and other resources is found in every non-industrial farming system. In particular, local wild food sources are used – freshwater or sea fish, small and large game animals, nuts, herbs and fungi. The natural resources of the land are also exploited, such as in the mining of stone for tools.

Since people first came to Scotland they have been cutting,

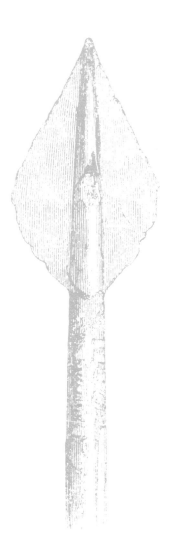

Coppiced Tree

How a coppiced tree is managed. When a tree, like hazel, is cut down, it will send up new shoots from the stump – these thin straight 'rods' can be used for making baskets and hurdles, hafting tools or making fences. The 'rods' can be cut every few years for a very long period – hundreds of years in some tree species. The rods begin to grow again straight away.

After Rackham

preserving and managing Scotland's forests. Farmers were then, as they have been throughout history, the main fellers of woodland, to clear land for agriculture. There is evidence that the hunter-gatherer-fishers were clearing hunting areas by fire, and they certainly used wood to make their tools and shelters. But they also learned very early to manage woods, to ensure consistent supplies of large forest-grown trees for building, and lighter wood for fences, firewood and wooden handles of tools, and so on. The lighter wood can only be guaranteed by active management of woodland, for example by coppicing. There is limited evidence in Scotland, but elsewhere in Britain we have evidence of Neolithic and Bronze Age people managing woodland for a number of different purposes – to make planks and beams, poles and pegs, bowls, baskets and other containers.

Where did farming come from?

The ultimate origins of the domesticated crops that formed the basis of farming in Britain lay in the lands bordering the eastern Mediterranean - the Levant, Turkey, the Balkans. Here the wild ancestors of modern cereal crops grew naturally in dense stands. Intensive use and management of these wild plants by hunter-gatherer-fishers led to the development of particularly useful and productive domesticated variants. Much the same processes governed the development of domesticated variants of sheep, cattle and pigs. As people managed these resources more and more intensively, a recognisable 'farming' system developed.

Farming as a way of life spread rapidly across central Europe – apparently by people moving to seek new land. By around 5000 BC the fertile soils of the major north European river valleys supported farming communities who lived in long timber houses, made pottery containers, cultivated wheat, barley, lentils and flax, and raised domestic cattle, pigs and sheep. In the westernmost areas, farmers may have been indigenous peoples who had adopted farming, rather than colonists. Somehow the actual domesticated animals and cereals, as well as the knowledge of how to manage them, and how to make pottery, were transported across the North Sea to the British Isles. However, we know very little about how farming was adopted by the hunter-gatherer-fisher communities of the north-west continental coast.

Local development or foreign import?

Precisely how farming came to replace hunting and gathering as the predominant way of life in north-west Europe and Britain is a matter of considerable argument. Nowhere in Britain have we yet discovered anything that looks like a farm or house-type transplanted from the continent to Britain. The best candidate for a structure built by incomers, although perhaps not by early generations, is at Balbridie near Aberdeen, which may be compared (but only in very general terms) to continental structures. However, very few sites have yet been excavated by archaeologists.

We do not fully understand how agriculture became the way of life of the majority of Britain's people. Was the existing population of hunter-gatherer-fishers replaced by an immigrant population from continental Europe? Did the local population adopt farming gradually, with little influence from abroad? The answer probably lies somewhere between - there were immigrants who brought the animals, equipment and ideas, but the local population began to adopt some or all of the ways of life, at different rates and in different ways, in the various regions of Scotland. It has been suggested that there were three stages in the change.

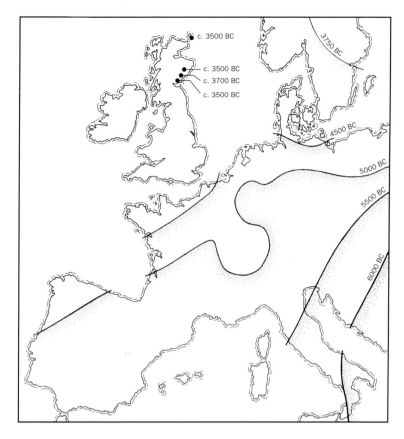

Farming Map

Map showing the approximate dates by which farming has spread across Europe.
After Bradley, Ammerman and Cavallo-Sforza, with the addition of radiocarbon dates from early Neolithic sites in eastern Scotland

Firstly, the idea of agriculture became apparent to hunter-gatherers, from contact with farmers, who had the necessary domestic animals and plants and the skills to use them. Then hunter-gatherer-fishers adopted some aspects of the farming way of life and so began the process of substitution of one economic system for another. And lastly, the change was consolidated and the economic system became wholly based on farming, with consequent changes to the social structure, making a 'return' to hunter-gathering impossible.

Recent studies show that hunter-gatherer-fishers across Europe may have been using plant resources quite intensively, managing them in such a way as to preserve and maximise the resource, in the centuries before farming became established.

A Neolithic Hall
In this reconstruction of the Balbridie building, everything above ground level is conjecture.
DAVID HOGG

Pots
Some of the pottery from Balbridie.
IAN RALSTON

Balbridie excavation

The early Neolithic building at Balbridie, during excavation.

IAN RALSTON

Balbridie

So far nothing similar to the massive building at Balbridie, Aberdeenshire, has been excavated in Britain, either in scale (it is 24 metres long and 10 metres broad) or style of construction, although broadly comparable cropmark sites are now known (including one on the opposite bank of the River Dee), but have not yet been excavated. Radiocarbon dating puts the building around 3900–3700 BC. The excavator of Balbridie commented that '. . . the farmers of Balbridie were – in terms of their building and, it would seem, of their strategy with cereals – closer to continental European practice than has normally been identified in the British Isles.' The building can be compared very generally to some examples on the continent, for example one at Flögeln, near Cuxhaven in northern Germany. The floor surface of the house has been lost to modern ploughing so there is no sign of a hearth. Consider-able quantities of charred grain (emmer wheat, bread wheat and barley) were found in some of the postholes. It is likely that the people living in the building also herded cattle and caught fish in the nearby river Dee. We have no real idea if the Balbridie building was a house in which perhaps an 'extended family' of three generations lived, or some sort of communal structure in the middle of a settlement of smaller houses, or an isolated building with a mainly ceremonial or religious function. However, it is entirely possible that the Balbridie building does represent a settlement built by people from the continent, or their close descendants.

Interestingly the pottery and cereal grain was concentrated in the western end of the structure, implying that different parts of the building were used in different ways or for different purposes.

This might have made the change to agriculture – the even more intensive use of plant and animal resources – easier to adopt. Even when farming had been adopted as the main food source in Britain, hunting and fishing continued to play an important part in most people's diet.

The Regional Dimension

Unfortunately, explanations of the Neolithic period in Britain have generally relied perhaps too much, on the results of work done in areas where most sites have been excavated - southern England, Yorkshire and Orkney. While the results of much of the work done in these parts of the country may be relevant to other areas, it is becoming clear, as more work is done elsewhere, that there is considerable variation from one part of the country to another in how farming began, and how the farming societies lived, worked, worshipped and developed. So, we cannot interpret the timber settlements of the Neolithic in Aberdeenshire using the results of the excavations on the stone buildings at Skara Brae, nor use Stonehenge and Avebury as models with which to interpret the religious life of other parts of Britain and Ireland.

The uplands

In upland Scotland many features built of stone and soil survive, particularly burial mounds. Here traditional archaeological field survey can locate and describe sites, and early antiquarians and archaeologists discovered and excavated many of them. The remains of houses and fields are far more difficult to spot, because of the lack of any upstanding elements such as a bank or ditch, or cairn, and it is only recently that much work has been done on this aspect of life in the past. Sites that were made wholly out of timber (where only filled-in postholes will mark the site) will not normally be detected without excavation.

Cairn
The chambered cairn at Cairnholy, Dumfriesshire.
HISTORIC SCOTLAND

The lowlands

In the well-drained, easily-cultivated soils of the lowlands, where human settlement has always been densest, from the time of the hunter-gatherers to the present day, the remains of past peoples have very often been removed or flattened by later agriculture. Although many sites survive here surprisingly well, we rely to a great extent on aerial photography, which in the right conditions can reveal the remains of archaeological sites no longer visible on the surface. These sites would have been built not with stone, but with turf and timber. Over centuries and millennia they have fallen down and been ploughed flat.

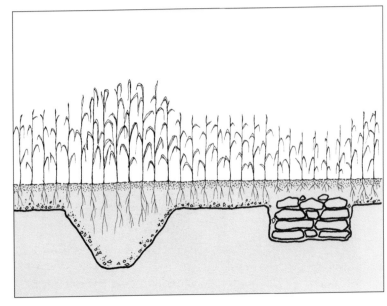

However, aerial photography will only detect sites where fairly substantial pits and postholes have been dug - it is features such as these that produce the marks, known as cropmarks, on aerial photographs. Structures built using shallow postholes, or erected wholly on the ground surface, cannot normally be detected from the air.

Serious archaeological aerial photography only began in Scotland in the mid 1970s, but the results have transformed our understanding not only of the Neolithic, but of prehistoric Scotland as a whole. We now know that thousands of sites not made of stone survive beneath the ploughed fields of lowland Scotland.

Little evidence has been found in southern England for Neolithic houses or arable farming. Many archaeologists working there feel that this evidence should have turned up by now if it existed. The conclusion they draw is that as no houses or fields have been found, few or none existed and that the Neolithic way of life was therefore mobile - for example people might have moved around with their herd of cattle, living in tents or other portable structures. Their view of the Neolithic may well be valid for southern Britain, but some of their arguments have been transferred wholesale to northern Britain, where they may be inappropriate. These archaeologists may be taking too little account of the evidence for houses that has appeared in other parts of the British Isles, and of the threats to the survival of the remains of these possibly slight timber buildings in intensively cultivated areas, where generations of farmers have ploughed and reshaped the land on which they stood.

Cropmarks

How cropmarks are formed. In dry weather the cereal crop grows taller, and stays green, over the topsoil fills of a ditch, which holds water. The ditch shows up on aerial photographs as a green line of higher plants, against the ripe golden crop. Over the wall, in contrast, the crop has less water, and falters and whitens. *After Wilson*

Round Barrow

The Neolithic round barrow at Pitnacree.

Long Barrow

The barrow at Longmanhill. The burial mound seems to have been built in two stages – first, a round mound, then a long 'tail' added. The boundary between the two is marked by a dip.

The Early Neolithic

Our modern world separates daily life from religion or ritual to an extent that would be incomprehensible to a farmer in the Neolithic period. In most non-industrial societies all aspects of life, from the processes of farming to the choice of a marriage partner, from the treatment of illness and death to the relationships between and within families, are bound together by custom, mutual obligations, ritual and religion to a far greater extent

Long Cairn
A ceremony in the forecourt of a long cairn.
HISTORIC SCOTLAND

than in our own society. For convenience, we can consider ritual and religion in two ways. First, the normal everyday observances that structure daily life (such as saying grace before a meal), and the 'set-piece' religious or ritual occasion, when special places may be used and larger than normal gatherings of people come together (such as a wedding or a funeral).

Our understanding of Neolithic society in the British Isles is based largely on interpretations of the many burial and ceremonial structures that survive, and the changes over time in the way these places were used. We have far less information about the day-to-day life of these people, and of course no written evidence.

Tombs of the ancestors

The most prominent and widespread remnants of the first farmers are their burial mounds, built out of timber, turf stripped from the surrounding areas, soil and subsoil dug from ditches immediately beside the mounds, and stone cleared from fields. Over most of Britain the burial mounds of soil and stone are long, but in some places (Yorkshire and Perthshire/Angus for example) they are more often round. In much of lowland Britain (in eastern and south-western Scotland, the east and south-west of England) the mounds, whether long or round, tend to cover broadly similar complex timber mortuary structures. In other areas (in Scotland, the west, the Northern Isles, and once again the south-west), a perplexing range of stone-chambered tombs was built, reflecting practice in different areas and at different times. The major difference between the timber and stone mortuary structures is that the stone chambers could be re-entered, perhaps

Mortuary Structure

A reconstruction of how a linear zone mortuary structure might have looked in use.
DAVID HOGG

Burial Chamber

The stone burial chamber of a tomb as drawn in the 19th century.

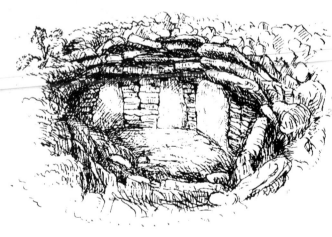

repeatedly, to bury more bone; in contrast, the wooden chambers were probably used for repeated interment of bone only while they were free-standing structures: they seem only to have been covered with mounds at the end of their use. Much ink has been spilt over the meaning of the different shapes of the stone chambers, but it has hardly advanced our understanding of the nature and use of the tombs.

Excavation of burial sites usually demonstrates one thing in common - the burial of numbers of bodies together. Often the bodies have either been defleshed before they were buried or the bones have been re-arranged later; for example, the long bones of a number of individuals being placed together in one part of a tomb, with skulls in another part. This has been interpreted as indicating that in death, people were not represented as individuals, but as part of the communal mass of 'ancestors' - taken further, this has been thought to show that the society that built these tombs was one in which individual differences in status were played down. This is in contrast to the late Neolithic, when there is evidence that this attitude changed.

Defleshing bodies prior to final burial has been practised widely. In many societies studied around the world in the recent past, death is seen as more complex than the difference between the human machine working, and then not working. Some peoples consider that there is an intermediate phase, lasting as long as the body still has flesh on it, where the spirit of the dead person is still in transition from life to death - at this time the spirit is often seen as dangerous to the living, particularly to the spouse or close relatives. Defleshing therefore may be hastened by exposing the body to animals or to birds - a process known as 'excarnation', or by putting it in a temporary grave for some months. At the end of this process the defleshed body is usually given a final burial.

In Britain we have some evidence of excarnation. At Hambledon Hill in Dorset, part of the Neolithic enclosure complex seems to have been given over to excarnation; in one case the pelvis and upper leg bones of a man ended up in a ditch, after being gnawed and dragged round by dogs. Exposure to birds was perhaps more efficient, in that the main portions of the body were more likely to remain where one left them, although small parts such as finger and toe bones might be removed. However, to ensure that the body is not disturbed by larger creatures, a more elaborate structure is needed to protect the corpse. A possible exposure site is known at Balfarg in Fife, where two small timber enclosures had surrounded a sequence of two- and four-post structures, interpreted as platforms for exposing human remains.

Rectangular ditched enclosures identified first in southern England have been interpreted as being related to these burial traditions because they are similar to long barrows in size, shape and date. They are usually called 'long mortuary enclosures'. One such site excavated at Inchtuthil in Perthshire measured 50 metres by 10 metres and dates to about 3900 BC. A fence of posts and hurdles had been set up in the ditch, and at some time later had been set on fire. While it was still burning, it had been pushed over and gravel and soil dumped on top of it. Ploughing, however, had removed all trace of what had happened inside the enclosure, or any covering mound, and we cannot tell if the site was actually used in the disposal of the dead.

Avenues of power: cursus monuments and bank barrows

Although the burial mounds of the early Neolithic were substantial earthworks, they appear relatively insignificant in relation to two other types of monument being built in the early Neolithic - cursus monuments and bank barrows. Both kinds of monument appear to be related to the tradition of the long barrows, but seem designed to make a far greater 'statement' in the landscape. There are few reliable radiocarbon dates for either cursus monuments or bank barrows, but it seems likely that their construction started later in the early Neolithic.

Cursus monuments were so named in the eighteenth century by early archaeologists because they looked liked Roman chariot-racing tracks (*cursus* in Latin). Most cursus monuments in England, where they were first discovered, are long, rectangular ditched enclosures, the longest being the D_____ cursus, 10km and 100m wide. In most, the soil dug from ___ ditch was piled up on the inner edge of the ditch.____

All but one of the 30 or so S_____ cursus monuments appear as cropmarks, defined either by d_____ at Holywood (Dumfriesshire), or - a Scottish va____ - by parallel lines of pits, as at Balneaves, in Angus. At Bannockburn, Stirlingshire, two sites defined by pits were excavated; one consisted of simple pits, in the other the pits had held posts. Although all these sites were

Exposure Platform
A North American Indian platform for the exposure of the dead.
PETER YEOMAN

Cursus Monument
An aerial photograph of one of the cursus monuments at Holywood.
RCAHMS

clearly related to the same tradition, it is difficult to suggest that they all had the same purpose.

Bank barrows are also very long, up to 2km. They appear to be grossly exaggerated versions of normal long barrows. There is clear evidence that cursus monuments and bank barrows are related – not least because in Scotland we have one monument that appears to be both cursus and bank barrow – the Cleaven Dyke.

Other aspects of the religious lives of the early Neolithic people were represented by less obvious structures than burial mounds, cursus monuments and bank barrows. There is consistent evidence that some sort of ceremonial activity involved the placing of, most often, burnt and broken pottery, but also stone tools and possibly organic material, in pits; the material is not thrown in, as if it were rubbish, but placed carefully, for example, lining the edge of the pit, or sealed under a carefully laid layer of stone.

Distribution Map
The distribution of cursus monuments and bank barrows in Scotland.

Douglasmuir Cursus
The cursus-type enclosure at Douglasmuir under excavation; the pits held massive oak posts. It was almost certainly built in two phases, one compartment after the other.
HISTORIC SCOTLAND

Opposite
Cursus Under Excavation
One of the Holywood cursus monuments under excavation. The dig revealed that the ditch had been re-excavated after it had filled in, and a screen of postholes was placed across one of the entrance gaps. RCAHMS

Cleaven Dyke

How the Cleaven Dyke probably looked during construction, over 5000 years ago.
DAVID HOGG

The Cleaven Dyke

The one Scottish cursus monument which does not appear as a cropmark is the Cleaven Dyke, Perthshire, which runs for over 2km. The central portion (1.8 km long) survives as a visible earthwork - a 9m wide bank, standing 1-3m high, running midway between two ditches, 50m apart. The construction of the Dyke has been dated to around 3300 BC.

Detailed survey of the monument has shown that it was built in five main sections, separated by breaks in the bank and ditches, and subdivided within the sections into about 34 segments. The boundaries between segments are marked by dips in the height of the bank and by narrowing of the ditches at the ends of segments.

The building of the Dyke seems to have started at the north-west end, where the first part was an oval burial mound (like Pitnacree, page 18). Then a long 'tail' was added; this looks like a normal long barrow of the period and with its quarry ditches beside the bank. Finally, the Cleaven Dyke proper, with its widely spaced ditches and central bank was added.

The apparent large scale of the effort necessary to construct the Cleaven Dyke may be an illusion; it, and other cursus monuments, may have been built over a long period, in relatively short segments. The 34 segments of the Dyke may reflect the number of years of construction; in other words, within two generations. In some societies coming together over a long period to repeat some ritual activity (in this case the construction of a segment of the Dyke) may be more important than the monument eventually produced by many years' labour.

Cleaven Dyke

The north-western end of the Cleaven Dyke had a complex building history - first, an oval burial mound; second a long barrow the ditches of which cut the edge of the earlier oval mound; finally the Cleaven Dyke proper, with its widely-spaced ditches, which continued for almost 2 km.
DAVID HOGG

OVAL BARROW

LONG BARROW

CLEAVEN DYKE PROPER

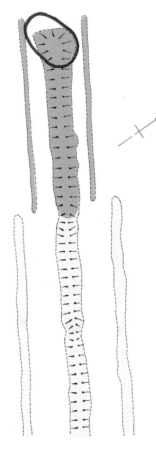

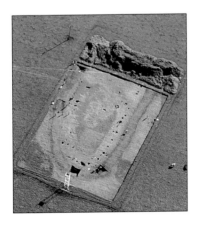

The farm

Where the evidence survives and has been investigated by archaeologists, it seems that the early Neolithic people in Scotland lived in small rectangular houses and indeed built their ceremonial structures in much the same shape. Excavations at Eilean Domhnuill, North Uist, have provided evidence of two roughly rectangular houses measuring 6.5m by 4m and 4m by 3m internally, and probably dating to around 3500 BC. They are similar to those found at Knap of Howar, Orkney, measuring 7.5m by 3m and 10m by 4.5m internally, where evidence of an economy based on arable agriculture in the form of cereal grains and querns and on a variety of wild resources, was also found.

These structures in North Uist and Orkney can be compared generally with surviving evidence in other parts of Britain and Ireland, for example the houses at Ballyglass in Ireland (measuring 7.4m by 6.4m) and the recently excavated house at Tankardstown in Co Limerick, both of which have produced dates around 4000 BC. The houses at Lismore Fields, Derbyshire, are of similar dimensions. Some of the houses mentioned recall aspects of Neolithic timber houses in continental Europe.

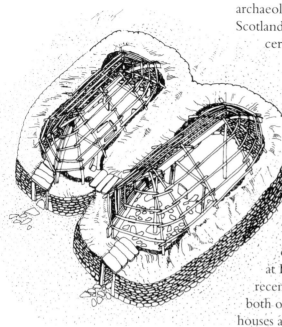

Knap of Howar

A reconstruction of the two houses at Knap of Howar, showing how the roofs were constructed.
HISTORIC SCOTLAND

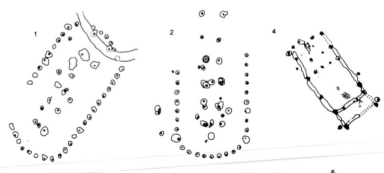

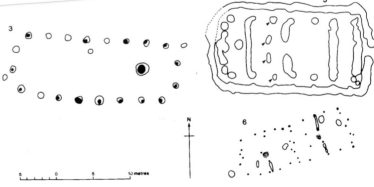

Plans

Plans of some Neolithic structures from Britain and Ireland - some roofed, others not. 1 & 2 - possible mortuary structures at Balfarg, Fife; 3 - ceremonial structure at Littleour, Perthshire; 4 - house at Ballynagilly, N Ireland; 5 - the vast building at Balbridie, Aberdeenshire; 6 - two houses built end to end at Lismore Fields, Derbyshire.

To date, the massive building at Balbridie, Aberdeenshire (page 15), has no excavated parallel in Britain, either for scale or construction.

In southern Britain there are many massive enclosures, dating from about 4000 BC to 3000 BC; these have been called causewayed camps, because the ditches and banks surrounding them are broken by many gaps. They seem to have served many purposes – settlement, defence and exposure of the dead. In Scotland, there is as yet no certain evidence for large-scale Neolithic enclosures to compare with these southern British sites, although an example has recently been found in Northern Ireland. There are hints of similar enclosures at Balloch Hill, Argyll and Bute (associated with Neolithic pottery), and at Carwinning Hill, Ayrshire, where causewayed ditches were recorded under later hillforts. The very limited excavation of a possible domestic enclosure at Kinloch Farm, Fife, has suggested there may also be a tradition of enclosed Neolithic settlement in eastern Scotland yet to be explored. Aerial photography has revealed possible causewayed sites, such as Leadketty, Perthshire; field walking here has produced flint tools of types used in the Neolithic.

As yet there is only limited evidence in northern Britain of the warfare seen on sites in the middle part of the Neolithic in southern and south-western England, where large fortified enclosures were attacked and burned. In one striking case in Dorset, archaeologists found in the ditch in front of the fort wall, the skeleton of young man who had been shot in the back with an arrow, while running holding a child.

The excavation of the Neolithic settlement at Knap of Howar has provided a useful picture of the nature of settlement and range of resources being exploited around 3500 to 3000 BC. There is evidence of cereal cultivation (grinding stones and cereal grains and pollen), and of cattle and sheep or goat. There is also evidence for some pig keeping, limited use of wild animals for wood (deer, seal, whale, otter), and more intensive exploitation of sea birds, fish and shellfish. At Knap of Howar there is also evidence of the collection of seaweed, perhaps as manure or food (for animals or humans), or for use as thatch (as was common in Orkney until recent times).

Leadketty
Aerial photograph of the massive enclosure at Leadketty, near Perth; the considerable number of breaks in the ditch suggests a relationship with the causewayed camp of England. There is another, undated enclosure, to the left. Flint tools found in the topsoil are of Neolithic date.
RCAHMS

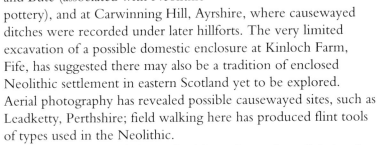

A model that might be useful in the interpretation of the available information is crofting, which also used intensively a wide range of wild and domesticated resources. This model of a small-scale, intensive, subsistence economy which made use of a wide range of resources may be more helpful than previous comparisons made with later large-scale prehistoric agricultural systems in southern England. More recent farming communities have managed very well using hoes and spades for cultivation - it has been written of more recent spade cultivation in Scotland: 'Twelve men using *caschroms* [foot spades] could till an acre a day, and a season's work with one from Christmas till late April or May could till enough ground to feed a family of seven or eight . . . for a year'.

There is evidence for enclosures or fields in the early Neolithic - at Shurton Hill on Shetland, for example, a stone dyke seems to have been built around pasture land soon after c. 3600 BC. What was being grown in these fields and plots? Direct evidence for cultivated cereals is limited for both the early and late Neolithic. Evidence for both barley and wheat was recovered from the settlement at Knap of Howar, Orkney. At Balfarg, Fife a carbonised barley grain was found incorporated within an early Neolithic pottery sherd; this was radiocarbon dated to around 3600 BC. At Boghead, Moray, around 4000 BC barley made up 88 per cent of the cereal grains, and emmer wheat 11 per cent. The material from the timber building at Balbridie, broadly contemporary with Boghead, has added considerably to our knowledge. Emmer wheat made up a large component (almost 80 per cent) of the cereals found, barley 18 per cent and bread wheat 2 per cent. Other, non-food, plants were also used, for example cultivated flax at Balbridie. Our Neolithic ancestors therefore probably worked for part of the year in productive plots, cultivated using hoes and spades, possibly with ards to cut up the ground surface; the cultivated areas were perhaps of considerable extent; the organisation, size and boundary structures of such plots or fields might vary widely, from permanent arrangements to areas re-defined frequently by shifting hurdles or even slighter demarcations, depending on local practice and land tenure arrangements. There is evidence for managed pasture under the long barrow at Dalladies, Angus, and under the Cleaven Dyke, Perthshire.

Although there is no direct evidence for 'transhumance' - the process of moving cattle, sheep or goats to high pastures in the summer - in the Neolithic, the practice has a very long history in Europe. The recent Scottish tradition of transhumance, the occupation of the shielings in the

Cup-and-ring Markings
Complex cup-and-ring markings, from Aberdeenshire, discovered during the construction of farm buildings.
ANN MILES: HISTORIC SCOTLAND

summer, only finally died out within living memory. However, it has been suggested that the distribution of cup-and-ring marks is related to transhumance. Recent work on the location of cup and ring marks in Perthshire and Dumfries and Galloway suggests that the more complex patterns are grouped in upland areas, around basins or waterholes, or on isolated hilltops and on routes to upland pastures, although for no purpose that we can at present determine. Cup and ring marks are found first in the early Neolithic. Most, on standing stones, stone circles, in burial cists and on rock outcrops, were probably made in the late Neolithic and Bronze Age.

Axes and pots

During the Neolithic, resources were exploited, sometimes on a considerable scale, for the manufacture of tools and other items. There are examples in Scotland of the production of both stone axes and tools flaked from suitable stone, such as flint and chert. Four distinct groups of Scottish axehead rock have so far been identified by analysis of axes in museums, but to date only the exact location of one quarry has been found in Scotland, at Creag na Caillich in Perthshire, where quarrying went on in the late Neolithic.

The processes of quarrying and distribution raise many questions about the function, or range of functions, of the axes. The process of manufacture was once seen as a simple, almost industrial, process; only in recent years have we begun to appreciate its true complexity. For example, both of the quarries which have recently been examined in detail (Creag na Caillich and Langdale, Cumbria) are situated in striking locations with commanding views over the valleys below. The rock was quarried from the least accessible parts of isolated outcrops, not from the most easily available, suggesting that the choice of quarrying site was not wholly pragmatic, perhaps implying that the extraction areas were the preserve of privileged people.

Stone axes of this period range greatly in size and in quality of finish. Many are too small to have had a function as a cutting or digging implement, or are made of special materials (such as jadeite, the axes being imported into Scotland), are very finely finished and are either unsuitable for actual work or show no signs of having been used. Axe-shaped stones therefore may be functional or symbolic. It is in the latter role that axes may have been distributed over considerable distances, perhaps used in formal exchanges between individuals or groups.

Polished Axe
This highly polished, unused axe seems almost certain to have been purely symbolic.
NATIONAL MUSEUMS OF SCOTLAND

Creag na Caillich
The axe quarrying site at Creag na Caillich seems to have been chosen more for its prominence than for its ease of access.
NATIONAL MUSEUMS OF SCOTLAND

Flint Axe
The flint axe seems to have been of practical use.
NATIONAL MUSEUMS OF SCOTLAND

Pottery is one of the characteristic features of the Neolithic in Britain. Containers in earlier periods may have made of bark, skin or basketry. It may be that pottery has more than a simple pragmatic meaning – the transformation of a simple natural substance (clay), through skilled manipulation and fire, into a shaped, often decorated, hard, smooth and clearly non-natural pot, would have been a striking achievement to people not previously acquainted with it.

Throughout the Neolithic and Bronze Age people in different parts of Britain made pottery that varied in style and decoration, expressing their own local traditions. In the early Neolithic all pottery was round-bottomed, but varied greatly in shape and decoration.

Pots

A range of earlier Neolithic pots from different regional traditions.
DAVID HOGG

The Late Neolithic

There are many reasons to believe that there were significant changes in society over most of Britain starting around 3300 BC in Scotland. There was already evidence of increasing diversity from place to place in burial and religious practice, and as the changes progressed, even greater regional diversity can be detected. The construction of the cursus monuments (which may begin later in the early Neolithic, although this is not clear), indicates a change away from the society that built the communal burial mounds, the construction of which ended in most parts of Scotland around 2500 BC.

In most areas late Neolithic burials (where limited evidence survives) are more likely to be of individuals rather than of a mass of anonymous bone from several people; it may be that it was now possible for the status of prominent individuals to be reflected in the way they were buried; for example, occupying a tomb designed solely for them. At much the same time a completely new type of ceremonial site – the henge – was built.

Henges

We do not know what went on in enclosures of the kind known as henges, but they are generally accepted to be places in which religious ceremonies took place. They normally comprise a ditch with external bank, the purpose of which may have been to screen the interior from view (suggesting that only a select few took part in what went on in the interior); there are usually one or two entrances and often there are settings of timber or stone uprights. Enclosures that can be interpreted as being henges or

Cairnpapple Henge
How the henge monument at Cairnpapple might have looked when it was being built.
DAVID HOGG: HISTORIC SCOTLAND

North Mains Henge

The classic henge monument at North Mains, Perthshire, under excavation.

HISTORIC SCOTLAND

related to the henge tradition vary in diameter from less than 10 metres to almost 400 metres in diameter (the largest being found only in southern England); the smallest (below 20 metres) are called hengiform enclosures. Stonehenge, although providing the origin of the name, can now be seen probably to be more a development of the southern British causewayed camp tradition.

More work was required to construct a substantial henge than an early Neolithic burial mound, but less than for a cursus monument like the Cleaven Dyke. However, the construction of the Dyke, and possibly other cursus monuments, was undertaken over a prolonged period; the henges were presumably built in a single operation. The amount of labour and the organisation necessary to construct the medium and large henges has been used to support the view that in the late Neolithic a more hierarchical society was developing, indicated by the appearance of single burials (possibly of 'chiefs') already mentioned. Such a society, where larger numbers of people were grouped together under the sway of an individual or family, might have a need for large-scale gatherings of the kind implied by the large scale of henge enclosures. However, many of the Scottish henges are small, and would have required less effort than the construction of one of the earlier burial mounds.

The point at which the organisation of religious life around burial mounds (characteristic of the early Neolithic) began to give way to the late Neolithic ceremonial enclosures - the henges - may have been detected by archaeologists at two sites in Scotland, at Maes Howe in Orkney and at Balfarg in Fife. At Maes Howe, the tomb (see page 40), part of a late local survival of the communal burial tradition, was encircled by a ditch and bank which has been compared to a henge; a further possible example has been recognised recently by Richard Bradley, at the tomb of Reay of Bookan, Orkney. Two 'true' henges were constructed nearby, at Stenness and the Ring of Brodgar. At Balfarg, Fife, a structure possibly used in the exposure of bodies

prior to communal burial in the early Neolithic tradition was, at the end of its use, covered by a low mound of earth and surrounded by a henge. Both mound and ditch contained Grooved Ware pottery; the ditch deposits were dated to around 3100 BC. Perhaps such sites had to be altered to underline the change in ceremonial practice then underway – the same sort of thing happened when the church 'Christianised' henges and stone circles by building churches within them or enclosing them in churchyards or using them as cemeteries.

Wormy Hillock Henge
One of the smallest henges - the site at Wormy Hillock, Aberdeenshire.
HISTORIC SCOTLAND

Grooved Ware

Another strand of evidence in interpreting the late Neolithic period comes from a completely new type of pottery - Grooved Ware, which has often elaborate decoration in the form of scored grooves or applied ridges. In much of Britain it is found mainly in the new ceremonial sites, but in Orkney it is found also in the settlements of the period, although often for special uses (for example, as at Barnhouse, pages 37 – 39). Grooved Ware is found in Orkney, Tayside and Fife, and south-west Scotland; in England it is found in Wessex, East Anglia and Yorkshire. The gaps in the distribution (for example there is one isolated findspot at Raigmore in Inverness) may be the result either of real original differences in distribution, or of the amounts varying of archaeological work undertaken in different areas of Britain.

Pottery

Pottery of the Grooved Ware tradition. DAVID HOGG

There are also other styles of late Neolithic pottery, heavily decorated, but we know even less about how and where they were used than we do about Grooved Ware.

At Balfarg Riding School one of the larger Grooved Ware vessels found in a henge contained a substance based on black henbane (a member of the hemlock family), possibly used as an hallucinogen. Recent work has suggested that the some of the decorative patterns used on Grooved Ware may have originated in patterns seen by people in trance states brought on by using hallucinogens.

The radiocarbon dating evidence for the introduction of henges and of Grooved Ware consistently points to their use earlier in northern Britain than elsewhere, and it may be that whatever initiated these changes in society also began here.

Regional variation – late Neolithic stone circles

While henges are the typical large public monuments of the late Neolithic, a very different type of site is characteristic of north-eastern Scotland - the recumbent stone circle.
Ian Shepherd has argued that the construction of these circles

began in the late Neolithic, as early as 3000 BC. There are about 100 of these known in the relatively small area of the modern local authority area of Aberdeenshire. These sites comprise a ring of stones, around 20 metres in diameter with, in the south, or south-western arc, a large (sometimes very large) stone lying on its side (the 'recumbent' stone). This stone is almost always flanked by the two tallest stones in the circle, the height of the rest reducing towards the part of the circle furthest from the recumbent stone. In the 1970s it was suggested that the axis of the circle, looking over the recumbent stone, was aligned on points where the moon rose and set at its 'standstills' (the moon sets at different points along the horizon, depending on the place in its cycle – where the setting point stops moving in one direction, and changes to the other, is the 'standstill'). Since then careful study of the sites on the ground has suggested that it was the midsummer full moon in the sky that was important; therefore, rather than observation of the moon, we should perhaps consider that the moon, between the uprights and over the recumbent, was illuminating the circle. In the restricted area in which these circles occur there are very few henge monuments - only three, and all of them very small and unusual (see the map of the distribution of henges and recumbent stone circles on the next page). This means that, whilst in other parts of Scotland (and in much of mainland Britain) the henges – indications of communal construction and ritual - were being built, in the north-east the ceremonial monuments were completely different. Not only are they relatively small, but there are many of them; often two or three circles are in close proximity. Does this indicate that in this area society had not changed as it had elsewhere, and was still operating on the basis

Netherton
The recumbent stone circle at Netherton of Logie, as drawn by Fred Coles in the early years of the 20th century.

Castle Fraser Stone Circle
The recumbent stone circle at Castle
Fraser, Aberdeenshire.
HISTORIC SCOTLAND

The Midsummer Full Moon
A recumbent stone circle as it might been
used; the alignment of the sites suggests
that the time of the midsummer full moon
was significant in their design and use.
DAVID HOGG

of small groups of families rather than 'tribes' or 'chiefdoms'? This situation provides perhaps the clearest example of differences between regions, at least in traditions of monument building and ritual practice, in this period. It is interesting to note that no Grooved Ware, the pottery type found most often in henges, has yet been found in the north-east. The contrast in henge distribution between the north-east and Angus and Perthshire is particularly striking.

This impression of regional individuality given by the recumbent stone circles is further strengthened by the distribution of a distinctive type of find - the carved stone balls — which is also heavily concentrated within the same area.

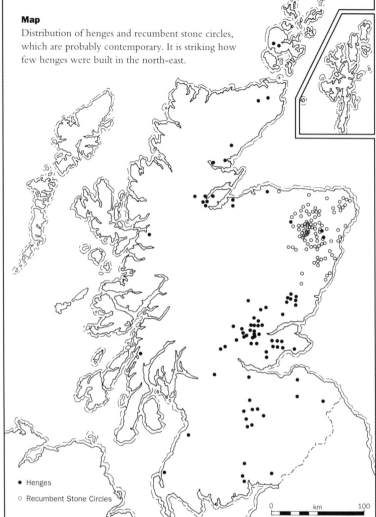

Map
Distribution of henges and recumbent stone circles, which are probably contemporary. It is striking how few henges were built in the north-east.

• Henges
○ Recumbent Stone Circles

0   km   100

In Arran, also in the late Neolithic, some of the impressive stone circles on Machrie Moor have been shown to have been built over the remains of earlier circles of upright timbers, associated with Grooved Ware pottery. At much the same time the impressive stone alignments at Calanais were being built, indicating another region's approach to the construction of ceremonial structures in the late Neolithic; here there was also an interest in the movements of the moon on the horizon. It is interesting to note that henge monuments have not yet been discovered in either Arran or the Western Isles.

Stone Ball
One of the enigmatic carved stone balls, most of which are from Aberdeenshire.
NATIONAL MUSEUMS OF SCOTLAND

Barnhouse Settlement

The village at Barnhouse, on Orkney, lies close to the two Orkney henge monuments - the Stones of Stenness and the Ring of Brodgar - within sight of Maes Howe. The settlement contains at least nine rounded late Neolithic houses, all with stone-built beds and dressers, of a kind generally familiar from the well-known settlement at Skara Brae, where, however, the houses are squarer and the stone-built fittings are not set in niches in the wall; the excavator of Barnhouse believes that the Skara Brae houses are later. At Barnhouse the walls only survive to a few centimetres high (although they have now been partly reconstructed). The houses all had stone-built drains. The walls at Barnhouse were probably built of turf and stone but it is not clear how the houses were roofed; the walls are thick enough to have supported a significant roof structure. In the reconstruction painting overleaf, the roofs are shown as being built on a wooden framework set at an angle of 40 to 45 degrees, covered with a thick thatch, probably of seaweed. In a wet and windy climate a flat or lower pitched roof would have been entirely impractical and would actually have been more difficult to build and maintain. The techniques assumed for the reconstruction survived in common use in north and north-western Scotland in simple farm and croft houses until relatively recently. There were signs that houses had been rebuilt on the same site a number of times. There was an open area at the core of the settlement, in which people had worked, making pottery, knapping flint and preparing hides for clothing.

One of the most exciting aspects of the Barnhouse excavation was that a fairly large part of the settlement could be investigated, showing that there were other types of structure in the village (this had also been noted at Skara Brae). In the south-west part of the village, there was a building ('house 2') that was very much larger than a normal house; it had two chambers instead of one, each with a central hearth. Like the smaller buildings it had bed recesses and a place for a recessed dresser. Interestingly, access to the inner chamber could only be obtained by going right round the hearth in the outer chamber. The excavator of Barnhouse, Colin Richards, has written compellingly about the parallels to be drawn between the layout of the late Neolithic houses of Orkney and other, more recent, societies in the way houses are laid out and used. Certain areas may be given over to different people - male or female, old or young, parent or child. Also, the way that houses are set out may reflect broader beliefs about the relationship of people to their world.

Opposite the entrance to the largest house is an even more impressive structure, which probably dates from soon after the abandonment of the rest of the settlement. The structure consists of a wall that encloses an area, over 20 metres across, which contains a large squarish building, more similar to the houses at Skara Brae than to the rest of the Barnhouse buildings. To enter it one would have had to walk over a hearth (one hopes without a fire lit on it!) - once again stressing the apparent symbolism of the hearth already seen in the two-chamber building. In the centre of the enclosure building was another hearth, behind which was the dresser commonly found in the normal houses; here, however, it was not in a recess, and looks more like a Skara Brae layout. All in all this was a strange building, especially when one considers how similar it (and some of the features of the other houses) is in layout to the Maes Howe type of tombs, and to the layout of the Stenness henge (which has a large paved area - intended to resemble a hearth? - at its centre).

Within the enclosure, a Grooved Ware pot containing traces of barley was found set in the ground up to the neck. We can only guess at the significance of this deposit.

Barnhouse Plan
Plan of the settlement at Barnhouse; the large structure at the bottom was probably built after the rest of the settlement had been abandoned. *After Richards*

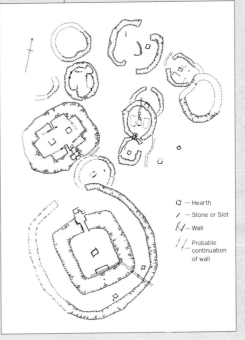

Thatch

Turf

Turf

Hearth

Door

Drain

Barnhouse Settlement

How the Barnhouse settlement may have looked. The reconstruction of the roofs – with a wooden frame at 40-45 degrees, covered by a deep thatch of seaweed – is based on more recent buildings in the northern isles. A flat roof would have needed more substantial timbers, and would have been very unstable in a windy environment.

Inset illustration *(left)* is a cutaway drawing showing how the roof would have been built.

DAVID HOGG

Barnhouse Excavation

The settlement at Barnhouse under excavation.

COLIN RICHARDS

Stone Balls
Three carved stone balls from
Aberdeenshire.
NATIONAL MUSEUMS OF SCOTLAND

Calanais
Calanais – the most spectacular stone
setting in Scotland, as recorded in this
19th century antiquarian print.

Regional variation – Maes Howe and the late tombs of Orkney

Maes Howe Chamber
How the chamber of Maes Howe may
have looked in use.
HISTORIC SCOTLAND

In Orkney a series of massive, complex chambered tombs was
built by the people who used Grooved Ware. Of these, Maes
Howe is the best known and most impressive – it is one of the
greatest architectural achievements of this period in Britain. Why
the use of massive communal burial structures continued into the
late Neolithic in this part of Scotland, when they were no longer
being built in the rest of Scotland, is unknown – it hints at
significantly different social structures at the time here, as do the
recumbent stone circles in north-east Scotland.

   The Maes Howe type tombs are not simple heaps of stones –
the visitor can see easily that the chambers and cairns of this
group are beautifully and impressively constructed. The tall
steep-sided 'core cairns' around the chamber, which are a

necessary part of the chamber, to support the stepped 'corbelling' roof, are very stable structures built of densely packed, horizontally-laid slabs, faced with good quality masonry.

Maes Howe
Maes Howe as depicted in the 19th century

The late Neolithic village

For archaeologists, Orkney provides the best settlement evidence for the late Neolithic, in particular from the excavated sites at Rinyo, Skara Brae, Links of Noltland and Barnhouse. The norm, different from what we know of the early Neolithic, seems to have relatively large-scale, communally-based settlement, occupied for long periods. In the earlier part of the period the houses were more free-standing (as at Barnhouse) - in the later village at Skara Brae the houses are more closely spaced, or even joined). Their inhabitants had a rich material culture and incorporated both mixed agriculture and intensive exploitation of wild resources, such as freshwater and sea fish. It appears that in Orkney and the Western Isles less easily cultivated, but more productive, clayey soils were exploited in the late Neolithic, following earlier exploitation of more easily cultivated land (which was however prone to drought in dry summers).

Maes Howe Plan
Maes Howe - plan & section of the chamber prepared for the Inventory of Monuments of Orkney in 1929.
RCAHMS

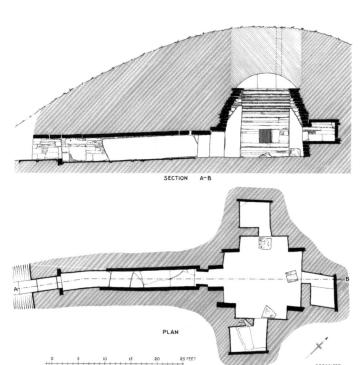

Boddam Den

Boddam Den, Aberdeenshire – how the
late Neolithic flint quarries may have
appeared in use.
DAVID HOGG

Calanais

The stone setting is only one phase in a complex sequence of use over many centuries

HISTORIC SCOTLAND

There may be a direct relationship between the development of Maes Howe type tombs and Grooved Ware and the economic and social innovations (including the development of larger scale settlements of the Skara Brae type) which allowed the communal effort necessary to exploit more difficult land.

Evidence of the use of 'ards' has been found at the Links of Noltland, Orkney; ards are simple cultivation implements, which were probably used to break up ground before cultivation using hoes and spades. At North Mains, Perthshire, a massive round barrow of the earlier part of the Bronze Age (before about 2500 BC) covered a surface that had been cultivated using narrow spade-dug ridges. Spade-dug ridges do a number of things - they improve soil drainage, they increase the depth of soil available for cultivation (on the ridges), and they increase soil warmth, all of which aid successful cultivation.

In Shetland there is evidence of land having been cleared and divided by walls between 3200 and 2800 BC. In Ireland there is evidence for very extensive and complex systems of fields, covering many square kilometres, by around 2800 BC. In some agricultural societies where land is held communally, cultivation plots may be marked in far less permanent ways, perhaps annually; for example, there is evidence of plots being divided by light fences in the late Neolithic on Arran, and by simple lines of hand-sized stones in the Bronze Age in Sutherland.

The balance of crops grown in the late Neolithic differed from those in earlier times – at Skara Brae, emmer wheat, the main crop at first, had declined to less than 10 per cent of the crop later in the Neolithic, and the decline continued into the earlier Bronze Age, in favour of barley. The actual size of emmer grains decreased at the same time, a sign of poor adaptation to the northern climate. Hulled barley, not represented in the early Neolithic at Boghead, Fochabers, was found in the late Neolithic at Skara Brae. A considerable use of wild resources is indicated at Northton, Harris, where 14 types of wild animals were found and at Noltland, Orkney, where 15 wild deer skeletons were recovered.

The more scattered late Neolithic settlement at Scord of Brouster in Shetland perhaps demonstrates that the sort of 'village' seen in Orkney was not necessarily the normal form of settlement throughout Scotland at this time.

Elsewhere in Britain the accidents of preservation have revealed only limited evidence of settlements, for example the two wooden buildings found under later burial mounds at Trelystan, Powys; the ground plans of these buildings are similar to those at Skara Brae, although they are lightly built of wood. While similar structures may remain to be found in lowland areas, it is probable that they will only survive, and be discovered, by chance.

At Meldon Bridge, Peeblesshire, is the only excavated example of a small, widely dispersed group of very large enclosures defined by massive posts, the postholes of which are clearly visible on aerial photographs. The sites are found as far apart as Forteviot in Perthshire and Dunragit, Dumfries and Galloway. The common characteristic is a narrow entrance passage formed of posts running out from the wall of the enclosure. At Meldon Bridge the timber fence cut off a promontory formed by the River Tweed and the Meldon Water, enclosing an area 10 hectares in extent. In the interior were found pits and postholes, possibly including traces of structures, associated with another type of late Neolithic pottery – 'impressed ware' – found over much of eastern Scotland. The enclosure had later been used for burial in the Bronze Age.

Two Pots
Two pots of the late Neolithic 'impressed ware' tradition.
DAVID HOGG

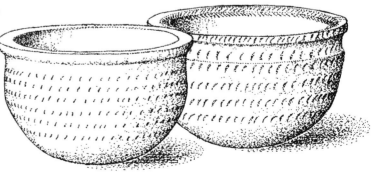

Equipment

Before metalworking was known, tools would have been made of wood and stone. Throughout the Neolithic wood was fairly easily obtainable over most of Scotland, but stone suitable for making sharp and strong tools is found only in certain areas.

Flint was the most commonly used stone for making tools – when struck it produces sharp edged flakes which can be used for cutting or scraping; larger pieces can be flaked and then ground into knives or axes. Clear evidence of large-scale late Neolithic flint extraction has been recovered from the Buchan gravels in Aberdeenshire; the largest known quarrying site is at the Den of Boddam, near Peterhead. Here both sides of a small valley had been ravaged by hundreds of intersecting quarry pits dug over several centuries to extract flint from the gravels. Radiocarbon dating places this activity in one part of the site between 3500 and 2000 BC. We do not know who dug the flint or how it was traded or distributed.

At Creag na Caillich in Perthshire, quarrying of stone for the manufacture of axes was being carried on around 2900 BC to 2300 BC. Axes made of stone from this site were widely distributed – one axe has been found as far away as Buckinghamshire.

Balfarg

The ceremonial complex at Balfarg, on the northern outskirts of Glenrothes New Town in Fife, is one of the most extensively investigated complexes of its kind in Britain. It was in use for over 1500 years, during which time it underwent many significant alterations, reflecting changes in practice and belief. The first recorded activity on the site was the digging of shallow pits, between 4200 and 3400 BC. In one of these pits, slabs of broken and burnt pottery were laid carefully round the edge; the pit was then filled and sealed near the top by a layer of stones. This kind of ritualised activity is a feature of much early Neolithic ceremonial activity.

Then two rectangular timber structures were built, probably one after the other, between 3700 and 3300 BC. These seem to have been fenced-off areas within which there were two- and four-post structures, possibly used for the exposure of the dead, prior to final burial. They are comparable with examples from other parts of the world.

One of the structures was certainly, and the other was probably, covered with low mounds of soil; the mounds contained Grooved Ware pottery, containing traces of black henbane, a plant used as a hallucinogen. The earlier structure had a ring cairn (a band of stone surrounding an empty central area) built over one end. The later of the two structures had a henge built round it. This could represent the conversion of a site associated with the earlier practice of communal burial to one associated with late Neolithic ceremonial activity.

Another henge was built a few hundred metres away; more Grooved Ware was found broken and burnt inside it. The henge enclosed a series of timber rings, which were eventually replaced by a stone circle.

At about the same time another stone circle was built to the east, at Balbirnie. In turn it was buried under a stone cairn.

Both henges, the Balbirnie stone circle, and the Balfarg ring cairn were later used for burials associated with Beakers and Food Vessels. One of the slabs of a cist at Balbirnie was decorated with cup and ring markings. Finally, many small deposits of cremated human bone were made on the Balbirnie stone circle and the ring cairn.

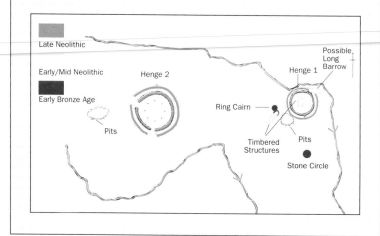

Late Neolithic

Early/Mid Neolithic

Early Bronze Age

Henge 2

Pits

Possible Long Barrow

Henge 1

Ring Cairn

Timbered Structures

Pits

Stone Circle

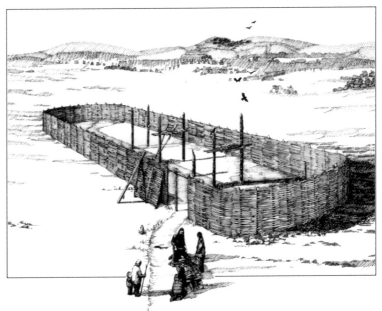

Ring Cairn – Balfarg
The ring cairn at Balfarg, built over the end of one the timber structures.
HISTORIC SCOTLAND

Balbirnie Stone Circle
Balbirnie stone circle, under excavation in 1970.
GRAHAM RITCHIE: HISTORIC SCOTLAND

Balfarg Structures
A possible reconstruction of one of the structures at Balfarg, as an enclosure and platforms for the exposure of the dead. See the North American Indian platform on page 21.
DAVID HOGG

Balfarg *(opposite)*
A simplified plan of the significant features of the ceremonial complex at Balfarg.
DAVID HOGG

Other stones suitable for flaking into implements - Arran pitchstone, Rhum bloodstone, chert and quartz - were also exploited, but the processes of their distribution are even less well understood.

As in the early Neolithic, goods were also exchanged between neighbouring groups - the most striking possibility being the carved stone balls already mentioned. The balls seem to have no intrinsic purpose, perhaps strengthening their interpretation as purely symbolic items.

Twenty years ago, Euan MacKie, drawing on the work of Alexander Thom (see p57), and on his own experience in the study of Mayan civilisation, argued that Britain in the late Neolithic was a theocracy, in which an elite of 'wise men, magicians, astronomers, priests, poets, jurists and engineers with all their families, retainers and attendant craftsmen and technicians' lived in major ceremonial complexes and in other special sites (such as all the known Skara Brae type settlements on Orkney). Fed by the efforts of a peasantry living in primitive conditions, this elite were supposed to undertake precise astronomical observation and set out their complex ceremonial sites using advanced geometry and a standard unit of measurement. His views have been dismissed by other archaeologists, who believe that the evidence shows a sophisticated and capable Neolithic farming society, not MacKie's society largely of primitive peasants run by a sophisticated elite.

Consolidating the hold: people and their environment

It is from the late Neolithic that we begin to see clear evidence of widespread and long-lasting clearance of woodland from the landscape (except Orkney and the other islands, which were not heavily wooded at any time), accompanied in some cases by significant soil erosion from the cleared land; for example, in the Bowmont Valley, Borders, the removal of trees for agriculture around 2000 BC seems to have resulted in catastrophic soil erosion. Many people would like to think that people in the past lived in a desirable equilibrium with their environment; however, examples of environmental damage caused by people in the past show that this is wishful thinking. In the late Neolithic results of pollen analysis were interpreted as showing a decline in the amount of land farmed, and a regeneration of woodland. However, it can as easily be explained by changes in the pattern of human settlement.

The Bronze Age

We must now deal with the change, real or otherwise, from 'the Neolithic' to 'the Bronze Age'. The first part of our journey into the past has been concerned with the establishment of a new way of life - farming, and the society that developed with and after that change. For much of the Neolithic and in most of the country certain unifying traditions could be detected, more strongly in the early Neolithic and weakening in the late Neolithic - the forms of burial in the early Neolithic, cursus monuments in the mid part of the period, and henges in the late Neolithic. In the Bronze Age the differences between regions become far more pronounced: although there may still be unifying traditions, and the way these are interpreted, for example in building of religious monuments and the way people were buried, becomes far more varied.

Until 30 years ago, virtually all changes within British prehistory were explained by 'invasions' of one people replacing another, rather than by changes within society. The Bronze Age was therefore seen as being the product of an 'invasion' by a separate group of people who used a special type of pot - the 'Beaker people'. But few would hold to such a view now.

'Magic Metal'
- the transformation of substances

It is perhaps difficult for us to understand just how amazing the process of working bronze would have seemed to people who had never seen it before. Copper ore would be transformed by heat into a shining pool of bright metal, and then by the smith's art and the addition of tin, into bright, shiny, hard and durable tools and ornaments. Throughout history metalsmiths have been seen as people apart, dangerous or powerful individuals; their power to transform substances must lie at the heart of this. Perhaps the occurrence of evidence of metalworking within many abandoned stone circles and henges, long after these sites had fallen out of use, indicates the religious awe which surrounded metalworking. Copper ores are widely available in Scotland, for example in Angus and Perthshire. No Bronze Age mines are yet known in Scotland, but at the Great Orme mine at Llandudno in Wales, a major complex of Bronze Age shafts and passages, has been investigated by archaeologists, and other mines are known in Ireland. Tin, the other important ingredient of bronze, is

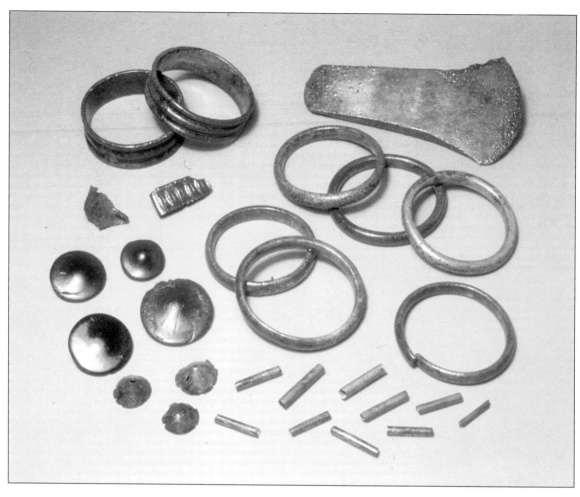

Bronze Age Equipment
A selection of early Bronze Age equipment.
NATIONAL MUSEUMS OF SCOTLAND

much rarer – Devon and Cornwall are the likeliest suppliers for the whole of Britain, although some tin may have come from mainland Europe.

The smelting of ore to produce copper requires very high temperatures – 1083 degrees Celsius. The ore is broken up into small fragments and placed in a small bowl furnace; charcoal is used as the fuel to heat it, blown to great heat by bellows. The molten metal collects in the bottom of the bowl. When it cools it can be re-melted in a crucible and then poured into moulds. Moulds and mould fragments are quite frequent finds on Bronze Age settlement sites in Britain as a whole. The finished tools could then be 'tinned' to give a shiny silvery finish, and polished, or ornamented by using gouges or punches,

Bronze Age people also worked gold into jewellery of great beauty. The gold, and most of the finished objects, probably came from Ireland, although there are naturally occurring gold deposits in Scotland, for example, in the Helmsdale River in Sutherland.

The creation of the metal tools and other equipment, particularly the larger, more decorative items, and the goldwork, was probably controlled by a limited number of people. We have seen that in the late Neolithic period changing burial practices, and the development of major ceremonial sites (the henges), perhaps indicated that individuals or families of higher status were increasingly playing a part in the organisation and control of society. It was perhaps these same groups who controlled the production and distribution of metalwork and other prestige goods. A society which uses artefacts as outward symbols of status and rank is likely to be competitive, because such symbols are open to imitation; effective maintenance of authority depends on control of manufacture and circulation of high-status objects.

'Powerful Pots'

Through the 19th century and for much of the 20th, the most commonly discovered features of the early Bronze Age were the burials - stone-lined graves (cists) containing one or, less often, more bodies, usually accompanied by a finely made pot, of the types called Beakers and Food Vessels (although both probably contained much the same sort of substances), or urns containing cremated bone. These pots were normally finely made and

Lunula
A gold lunula, or collar.
NATIONAL MUSEUMS OF SCOTLAND

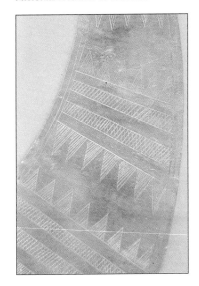

Lunula Detail
A detail of a lunula, showing the extraordinary workmanship.
NATIONAL MUSEUMS OF SCOTLAND

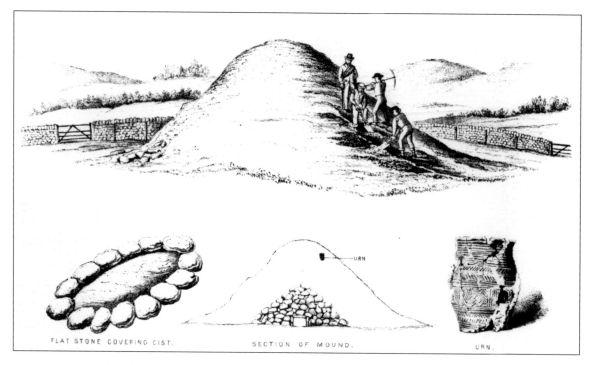

FLAT STONE COVERING CIST. SECTION OF MOUND. URN.

The Fairy Knowe of Pendreich A typical 19th century 'excavation' of a Bronze Age burial mound – the Fairy Knowe of Pendreich, 1867.

Bronze Age Cist Burial
A typical early Bronze Age cist burial; a woman aged about 25 at death, buried within the henge at North Mains, in around 2000 BC.
HISTORIC SCOTLAND

elaborately decorated. In most of Scotland they are found in burials, although they are also found on ceremonial or religious sites. In the Western Isles however, they turn up on settlement sites of the period – it may just be that we have not yet found these settlements in other parts of Scotland.

Although we have seen that in the late Neolithic period single burial was becoming common, the single burials we find still seem to be of special individuals – it is with the appearance of Beakers (at approximately the same time as the working of metal)

Bronze Age Pots A range of early Bronze Age pots from burials. Beakers, Food Vessels, an 'enlarged Food Vessel' and a collared urn. DAVID HOGG

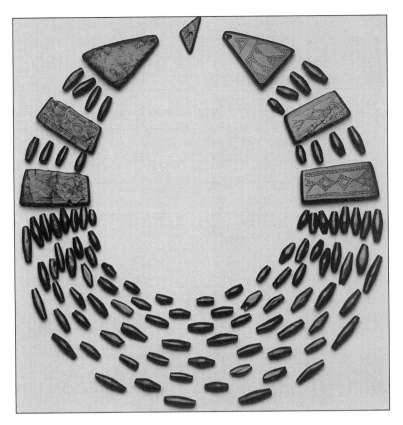

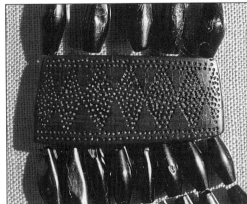

Jet Necklace
The jet necklace from the burial cist at Mountstewart.
NATIONAL MUSEUMS OF SCOTLAND

Necklace Detail
A detail, showing the workmanship on a jet necklace.
NATIONAL MUSEUMS OF SCOTLAND

and, later, Food Vessels that we have a more consistent form of burial that seems to provide for larger numbers of the population. At one time it was thought that there was a simple sequence - burials of bodies with Beakers, then with Food Vessels, and then a change of burial practice to cremation, with the burnt bone being placed in special urns. However, more recent excavation and radiocarbon dating confirms not only that Beakers, Food Vessels and urns may occur on the same site, possibly at much the same time (because Beakers went on being used for a very long time), but that other burial types are found there too - bodies in unlined pits, with or without pottery vessels, cremations in small pits, on occasion in cists with Beakers and so on. It has also become clear that many cemetery sites were covered by mounds, which have since been ploughed away. It may be that the type of burial a person received was more to do with who they were, or when they died, than with simple changes in tradition over a long period. At one cemetery in Fife a body had even been buried in a coracle which had been placed in a pit.

Recent work on analysing the pollen in the soils in the bottom of cists has shown that bodies may have been accompanied by flowers. However, many Beakers and Food Vessels have 'tide-marks' of crusty organic material showing the

Culduthel Grave Goods

The finds from the grave at Culduthel, Inverness-shire. The body was accompanied not only by the pot but by an archer's wristguard and eight flint arrowheads.

NATIONAL MUSEUMS OF SCOTLAND

original height of a liquid or semi-liquid material within them, possibly food or drink. Unfortunately, it is difficult to tell what pollen belongs to the flowers in the cist, and what relates to the material in the pots.

One of the other characteristic finds of the period, in particular in Beaker graves, is archery equipment - arrowheads and wrist guards - much of which is finely crafted. Although equipment made of flint, other stones, and metal may survive, the wooden parts of equipment of all kinds does not, except in rare circumstances - it is to this form of preservation that we owe what knowledge we have of the shafts of arrows or even of bows themselves. The only bow we have from the period we are considering in this book is from the early Neolithic, at Rotten Bottom in Dumfriesshire. That archery had more than ordinary significance is shown by two examples where arrows may have been used for the ritual killing of people who were then buried on sacred sites - one case at Stonehenge, and the other within a timber circle (accompanied by a Food Vessel) at Sarn-y-bryn-Caled, in Wales.

It is clear, however, that the relatively small-scale cists and cremations of individuals do not represent the whole spectrum of burial throughout the period. At North Mains in Tayside, a vast round mound 40 metres across and 5 metres high, proved on excavation to have a long and complex history.

First, the mound was set out on the ground using complex patterns of light wooden fences. There was a circular area in the middle, and fences radiating out forming a series of bays, like the slices of a cake. Then, the radial bays were filled with material dug from around the site, to create a ring bank with the central fenced area still open, and accessible from one side. One or more burials were placed in this area, and it was filled in. After this the mound was finished off to a more bowl-like shape, and a huge fire was lit on the top. Finally, the mound was smoothed off using turf, and a layer of stone was laid over the whole surface.

North Mains 1

The first phase of construction at North Mains saw the erection of a central timber enclosure, and many radial fences. Within the segments soil from the ditch was piled.

HISTORIC SCOTLAND: DAVID HOGG

Burials in cists were dug, at about the same time or later, into the surface.

Recent excavation and radiocarbon dating on the Clava cairns (named after one group of cairns at Balnuaran of Clava), near Inverness, seem to show that the cairns and their surrounding stone circles are broadly contemporary with North Mains, not several hundred years earlier, as was originally thought. The only surviving evidence of burial at a Clava Cairn (at Corrimony near Drumnadrochit) is a stain showing the position of the body of a single individual. It may be that all these massive round mounds of the early Bronze Age are indeed the burials of prominent individuals.

North Mains 2

At the end of the first phase of construction the mound at North Mains consisted of a stone and earthen bank surrounding an open central area, accessed by a passage. One or more bodies were buried in the central area, before 2000 BC.

HISTORIC SCOTLAND: DAVID HOGG

Clava Cairns
One of the Clava cairns as it appeared in 1860.

Stone circles

Stone circles are almost the definitive monument type of the Bronze Age. Many circles (for example, those within henge monuments and the Recumbent Stone Circles of north-east Scotland) can now be seen to date to the late Neolithic, but the majority of circles belong to the following thousand years, for they continued to be built until quite late in the Bronze Age. Modern excavations show that many stone circles were built on the sites of pre-existing circles of timber posts. We do not really know what went on the circles, although we speculate that they were used for communal ceremonies; what is very common,

Body Stain
The body stain in the chamber of the Clava-type cairn at Corrimony seems to be of a single individual.
STUART PIGGOTT

Clava Cairn The north-east cairn at Clava, under excavation in 1996. HISTORIC SCOTLAND

however, is that the circles were used for human burial late in their use, implying that they were sacred sites.

Astronomy and geometry

In the late 1960s a professional engineer, Alexander Thom, published surveys and interpretations of stone circles which he believed proved that the builders of the circles used complex geometry in setting them out, and used the circles for very detailed astronomical observation. At first his views and conclusions were dismissed entirely by the archaeological profession. However, more scientific survey and analysis of the results has confirmed that prehistoric people in Britain *were* interested in astronomical events and built their religious sites to align on them, but that they were not undertaking the precise observations suggested by Thom. The alignments used relate to major events in the annual movements of the sun and moon along the horizon, and the alignments are accurate only to within one or two degrees.

Thom's assertions that the stone circles were laid out using complex geometry, and a standard unit of measurement (the 'megalithic yard') have also been examined and found wanting. Studies of the geometry of stone circles rely on the application of very precise methods of analysis to monuments, often incomplete or altered during use, constructed of rough and irregular stones.

The fact is that geometry can be used to *describe* any shape that already exists, including any stone 'circle'. There is no proof whatsoever that complex geometrical processes were actually used to set out the shapes on the ground. Indeed, when exact geometrical shapes are applied to such sites, many of the stones

Edintian Stones
The 'four-poster' stone circle at Edintian in Perthshire, as drawn by Fred Coles in the early years of the 20th century.

will not lie on the theoretical line. It is more widely accepted that stone circles (many of which are not exactly circular) were laid out using simple methods, many by eye.

Settlements and environment

While the settlements of the Neolithic period are relatively rare, we know of far more settlements of the Bronze Age in Britain in general, particularly of the later Bronze Age. This is mainly because of the accidents of survival of sites. During the Bronze Age people were settling the uplands, perhaps because increasing population had resulted in a shortage of land in the lowlands. Because these areas have not been used intensively for agriculture in the two to three thousand years since, many settlement sites and indeed field systems survive. Other sites survive in sand dunes, as in the Western Isles. However, sites in the uplands and islands do not tell us what was happening in the lowlands, where sites have been ploughed flat and may appear, if at all, only as cropmarks.

Learable Hill Stones
The simple stone rows at Learable Hill, Sutherland. These are very simple, compared to some of the far more complex settings of Caithness. What any of the rows were for is a mystery.
HISTORIC SCOTLAND

Echt Stones
The stone circle and later kerb cairns at Echt, Aberdeenshire.
HISTORIC SCOTLAND

Unfortunately, few settlement sites of the Bronze Age have been excavated to modern standards and the amount of hard evidence remains limited. Therefore, while there are many house sites and associated field systems visible in much of upland Scotland, we cannot tell how many of them originated in the period we are discussing, up to 1500 BC; it is likely that most of the sites we can see on the hills are of a later period, covered in Richard Hingley's book in this series: *Settlement and Sacrifice*. On Arran, however, a hut circle was radiocarbon dated to around 1900 BC. Near Lairg, Sutherland, a long sequence of settlement from the early Neolithic (pits and pottery associated with

agricultural soils) to quite recent settlement was recovered by excavation. It included phases of intensive agriculture in the late Neolithic. The first houses to be found within the excavated areas (but presumably not the first in the vicinity) were round houses, dated to between 1750 and 1500 BC. In and around these substantial timber buildings were found pots, charred cereals, quern stones for grinding corn, and the stone tips of ploughs.

In the hills of southern Scotland we can see that a type of settlement more common in the late Bronze Age had its origins in the centuries before 1500 BC. These 'unenclosed platform settlements' appear as strings of circular platforms cut into the hillsides of the Borders and Clydesdale. The platforms were built to allow the construction of round houses. At Lintshie Gutter such houses were dated to around 2000 BC, the earliest dates yet obtained for round houses. There is evidence that the occupants grew cereals and tended flocks of sheep and herds of cattle.

Significant evidence for settlements of this period has been found in the Western Isles where two contrasting sites were excavated. At Rosinish, clear evidence for cereal cultivation was found – in the form of charred barley and oats, and the marks of ard-ploughing. However, there was only a small lightly built house. At Northton, in contrast, there were two more substantial houses, but no trace of arable farming. However, there was clear evidence for the use of domesticated animals (cattle and sheep) and hunting and fishing – the people had gathered and caught shellfish, seabirds, deer, lobster, crab, seal, and whale.

In the Northern Isles substantial buildings were erected on sites which had been occupied since the Neolithic, as at Scord of Brouster.

Houses, Fields and Cairns
An aerial photograph of an upland landscape - houses, fields and cairns - in Perthshire.
RCAHMS

A time of change

The period after that which we have been considering – the later Bronze Age – was a time of considerable change. It has been argued that this change was driven by a rapid and severe deterioration in the climate, which made mixed farming in the uplands impossible, forcing people to abandon their land. There have been claims that this was associated with major volcanic eruptions, but this is still a matter of debate. The period sees a considerable increase in the amount of bronze weaponry, and the establishment in many parts of Scotland of enclosed and, later, fortified settlements; both developments may relate to the

Bronze Age Round House

The reconstruction of an early Bronze Age round house.

HISTORIC SCOTLAND

shortage of land and people's efforts to take it by force or defend it. It is perhaps in this period that we can see the trend of the previous 3000 years reach a new stage of development - from an early Neolithic society in which overt expression of status was avoided in life and death, through the more hierarchical society of the late Neolithic, and finally to the fully-fledged tribal chiefdoms of the Iron Age.

As we move into the later Bronze Age, the construction of purpose-built monuments such as stone circles for special ceremonial purposes seems to decline, and the disposal of the dead becomes archaeologically less detectable – virtually no more cists or urns, no more cairns or burial mounds for over 1500 years. Perhaps here we see the beginnings of the later concerns with natural features - bodies of water and groves of trees – as places of worship.

Conclusions

The Neolithic and early Bronze Age, a period of over 2500 years, saw remarkable changes. Farming was established as the way of life of the great majority of the inhabitants of Britain, and we can see that these farming societies were capable of major works of design and construction, from great monuments to fine tools. Through their monuments, burials, settlements and possessions we can glimpse the richness and complexity of their daily lives and their religious beliefs. We can see also that these farmers were the ones who began the process of deforesting and smoothing the land - the people who began the processes that have led to our modern landscape.

Following page:
The Stones of Stenness
GORDON BARCLAY

How Do I Find Out More?

The remains of the Neolithic and early Bronze Age are scattered all over Scotland. Some areas have more that is both excavated and interpreted, but most areas have something worth seeing. The list is ordered by area, alphabetically. I have used a combination of the old region and the new local authority names – and have tried to give a broad geographical coverage, concentrating on monuments that are open to the public by Historic Scotland (marked HS) or by other bodies (marked P). Where there are no initials the site is on private land and the permission of the owner will be required. Ordnance Survey grid references are provided.

Aberdeenshire
Capo - (P) this enormous, well-preserved early Neolithic long barrow was not recognised until the 1970s. It stands in a large clearing in a Forestry Commission forest. NO 633 664.
Loanhead, Easter Aquhorthies, Tomnaverie - (HS) three recumbent stone circles. Loanhead and Easter Aquhorthies are particularly well preserved, while Tomnaverie has spectacular views over the Howe of Cromar. NJ 747 288; NJ 732 207; NJ 486 034.
Standing stones of Cullerlie - (HS) a complex Bronze Age stone circle with eight kerb cairns built within it. NJ 786 042.

Argyll
The Kilmartin Glen contains a remarkable series of burial and ceremonial sites (all HS):
Cup and Ring marked rocks - Achnabreck (NR 856 906), Ballygowan (NR 816 978), Baluachraig (NR 831 969), Cairnbaan (NR 838 910), Kilmichael Glassary (NR 857 934) - well preserved groups of marks.
Bronze Age and Neolithic Cairns - Dunchraigaig (NR 833 968), Glebe (NR 832 989), Nether Largie (3 cairns) (NR 830 983; NR 831 985; NR 828 979), Ri Cruin (NR 825 971).
Temple Wood stone and timber circles - NR 826 978.

Arran
Torrylin cairn - (HS) an early Neolithic long cairn. NR 955 210.
Machrie Moor - (HS) a spectacular group of five stone circles in a fine moorland setting. NR 910 324.

Auchagallon stone circle - (HS) a Bronze Age burial cairn surrounded by a circle of 15 standing stones. NR 893 346.

Caithness and Sutherland
The Grey Cairns of Camster - (HS) - two early Neolithic burial cairns - one long, one round - with spectacular chambers, now largely reconstructed after excavation. ND 260 441.
Cnoc Freceadain - (HS) two unexcavated long burial cairns with horned facades. ND 013 654.
Hill o' Many Stanes - (HS) one of the most complex of these enigmatic Neolithic or Bronze Age sites - multiple rows of small stones fanning out across the hillside. ND 295 384.

Dumfries and Galloway
Cairn Holy - (HS) two early Neolithic chambered cairns, one with a spectacular facade. NX 518 540
Drumtroddan cup and ring markings - (HS) three groups of well-defined marks. NX 362 447.

Fife
Balfarg - (P) elements of the early Neolithic to Bronze Age ceremonial complex, including a timber mortuary structure. The Balfarg henge and the Balbirnie stone circle have been laid out for visitors after excavation. NO 281 031.

Inverness-shire
Balnuaran of Clava - (HS) two Clava type passage graves and a ring cairn, each surrounded by a stone circle, and a kerb cairn, all of the Bronze Age. Examples of an unusual regionally restricted group of cairns. NH 752 439.

Corrimony cairn - (HS) a Clava cairn near Drumnadrochit, reconstructed after excavation. NH 383 303.

Lothians
Cairnpapple - (HS) - a complex site, with a henge, subsequently built over twice by burial cairns. The henge and outside of the cairns are accessible at all times. The site displays and the interior of the reconstructed cairn are open in summer. NS 987 717.

Moray
Quarry Wood henge - (P) a well-preserved henge monument of an unusual type. The ditch and external bank surrounding the enclosure are very narrow. The site lies in a clearing in a Forestry Commission Community Woodland. NJ 185 630.

Orkney
Orkney is the area in Scotland with the greatest number of visible Neolithic monuments; the few listed are a small selection.
Knap of Howar - (HS) a pair of stone-built houses of the early Neolithic, with cupboards. HY 483 519.
Maes Howe - (HS) this chambered tomb is the most striking example of Neolithic architecture in the UK. A large mound, surrounded by what may be a slightly later henge monument, covering a large stone chamber, reached by a long low passage HY 318 128.
Skara Brae - (HS) - spectacularly preserved late Neolithic village, with houses surviving to their full wall height and containing stone-built furniture. HY 231 188.
Barnhouse - (P) - the recently excavated

late Neolithic village lying close to Stenness, Brodgar and Maes Howe has been laid out for visitors by the Orkney Council. HY 306 124.

The Stones of Stenness and the Ring of Brodgar - (HS) - these two spectacular henges and stone circles overlook the Loch of Harry, close to Maes Howe and Barnhouse. HY 306 126 & HY 294 134.

Perthshire and Angus

Cleaven Dyke - the best preserved cursus monument/bank barrow in Britain. It survives for a length of 1.8km in woodland, crossing the main Perth to Blairgowrie road. The monument is owned by Meikleour estates, from whom permission to visit should be sought. NO 150 410 – NO 177 396.

Pitnacree - this early Neolithic round barrow can be seen easily from the roadside. NN 928 533

Carse, Dull - this 'four-poster' stone circle, although not open to the public can be appreciated from the roadside. When excavated in the 1970s a cremation in an urn was found within the setting. NN 802 487.

Croft Moraig - A complex double stone circle built on the site of an earlier wooden structure. NN 797 476.

Shetland

Staneydale 'Temple' - (HS) a large Neolithic building of stone. Heel-shaped on the outside, like the contemporary tombs on Shetland, with a large oval chamber within. The remains of a smaller building of the same period can be seen behind the path to the 'Temple', with contemporary field boundaries around it. HY 285 502.

Western Isles

Calanais (Callanish) - (HS) a spectacular complex setting of standing stones in an impressive situation. Excellent visitor centre run by local trust. NB 213 330.

Museums

Most local authority museums will have some Neolithic and Bronze Age material on display. However, some museums have particularly good collections of material from this period:

The National Museums of Scotland – the new Museum of Scotland is opening in Edinburgh in November 1998.

The Anthropological Museum, Marischal College, University of Aberdeen.

Tankerness House Museum, Kirkwall, Orkney.

Further Reading

Scotland: environment and archaeology 8000 BC to AD 1000, edited by Kevin Edwards & Ian Ralston (Wiley 1997). *Europe in the Neolithic,* Alistair Whittle (Cambridge University Press 1996). *Wild Harvesters: The First People in Scotland,* Bill Finlayson (Canongate 1998). *Settlement and Sacrifice: The Later Prehistoric People of Scotland,* Richard Hingley (Canongate 1998). *Neolithic & Bronze Age Scotland,* Patrick Ashmore (Batsford 1996). The *Exploring Scotland's Heritage* series (The Stationery Office), covers the whole of Scotland's prehistoric and more recent heritage in 9 regional volumes. *Altering the Earth,* Richard Bradley (Society of Antiquaries of Scotland 1993). *Archaeoastronomy,* Clive Ruggles (Yale 1998).

Acknowledgements

I am very grateful to the friends and colleagues who commented on drafts of this book – David Breeze, Richard Bradley, Elizabeth Goring, Alison Sheridan, and to Jackie Henrie for her editorial input. Thanks are due to the following individuals and organisations for their permission to reproduce their copyright illustrations: Historic Scotland; The Royal Commission on the Ancient and Historical Monuments of Scotland, National Museums of Scotland, Noel Fojut, Ian Ralston and Colin Richards. The illustrations on pages 11, 20, 33, 52, 56 and 57 appeared first in the pages of the *Proceedings of the Society of Antiquaries of Scotland.* The maps were prepared by Sylvia Stevenson and Rob Burns. The excavators of Balbridie (Ian Ralston), Barnhouse (Colin Richards) and Den of Boddam (Alan Saville) provided valuable input into the creation of the reconstruction paintings – the results, however, are my (and the artist David Hogg's) interpretation.

HISTORIC ⚑ SCOTLAND

HISTORIC SCOTLAND safeguards Scotland's built heritage, including its archaeology, and promotes its understanding and enjoyment on behalf of the Secretary of State for Scotland. It undertakes a programme of 'rescue archaeology', from which many of the results are published in this book series.

Scotland has a wealth of ancient monuments and historic buildings, ranging from prehistoric tombs and settlements to remains from the Second World War, and HISTORIC SCOTLAND gives legal protection to the most important, guarding them against damaging changes or destruction. HISTORIC SCOTLAND gives grants and advice to the owners and occupiers of these sites and buildings.

HISTORIC SCOTLAND has a membership scheme which allows access to properties in its care, as well as other benefits.
For information, contact:
0131 668 8999.